Original title:
Echoes of the Eerie Elm

Copyright © 2025 Creative Arts Management OÜ
All rights reserved.

Author: Riley Donovan
ISBN HARDBACK: 978-1-80567-371-2
ISBN PAPERBACK: 978-1-80567-670-6

Whispers in the Gloom

In the dark, a squirrel squeaks,
A tale of nuts and sneaky freaks.
Branches sway with laughter loud,
As shadows dance beneath the cloud.

A raccoon plays a prank on me,
He steals my lunch, oh can't you see?
With every rustle, giggles bloom,
In the mischievous whispers of gloom.

Shadows Beneath the Canopy

Beneath the boughs, a ghostly mime,
Pretends to dance through space and time.
A giggle here, a chuckle there,
Even the bats break out in flair.

With every twirl, they start to trip,
A lively scene, but oh, what a slip!
Laughter blends with the evening's sigh,
As shadows waltz beneath the sky.

The Haunted Grove's Lament

In the grove, old spirits boast,
Of midnight feasts and friendly ghosts.
They joke of hats and missing socks,
While the owls hoot as wise old clocks.

A lonely tree, it starts to sway,
As branches join in a funny play.
With every creak, a new joke born,
The spectral crowd laughs 'til the morn.

Secrets of the Timeless Tree

When nighttime falls, the stories stir,
Of playful winds and silly fur.
Old leaves chuckle, sharing their tales,
Of dancing lights and ghostly gales.

A wise old owl makes a wise-crack,
While shadows leap in a joyful pack.
The tree holds secrets, laughs in glee,
Of mischief that flows, wild and free.

Memories Lost in the Mist

In the fog, a squirrel sneezed,
And startled a mouse with a wheeze.
The owl hooted, then laughed out loud,
As shadows danced in the misty crowd.

Lost were the moments, they played a prank,
The rabbit made a banana bank.
Chasing dreams that got stuck in trees,
With giggles that carried on the breeze.

The Twilight Beckons the Bewitched

As twilight grinned with a crooked smile,
A witch tripped over her broom by a mile.
Her cauldron bubbled, the potion fizzed,
While bats debated how to be whizzed.

A ghost joined in with a silly jig,
He danced so wildly, he lost his wig.
They laughed as they floated through the night,
In a chaos of joy, what a sight!

Mournful Melodies from the Mulberry

In the branches, the birds sang wrong,
Their notes were more for a comedy song.
A cat in a hat pouted, then danced,
While the dog in the tree just pranced.

The berries wept purple tears for fun,
While the gossiping leaves had their run.
With every rustle, a chuckle they shared,
As the fruit dared to joke that nobody cared.

Tales of the Twisted Timber

The trees twisted tales with a mischievous twist,
Of woodpeckers who played hide-and-seek in the mist.
A raccoon in shades, sipping root beer,
Called out with laughter, "Come sit over here!"

The branches giggled as they swayed,
Telling stories where pranks were displayed.
And every stump joined the raucous cheer,
For the funny old woods held nothing to fear.

The Watchful Eyes of the Woodland

In shadows tall, the trees do peek,
With twigs for eyes, they hardly speak.
Squirrels chatter, oh what a sight,
Comparing their tails, a featherweight fight.

Mice in suits plan a grand parade,
While owls snicker, stay quite afraid.
Who will dance, and who will prance?
Caught in the whims of woodland romance.

Dreams of the Dreaded Timber

Bark so rough, it tells no lies,
While roots below can plot a surprise.
An acorn's dream is to be a tree,
But ants just laugh, "You'll never be free!"

Branches sway in a twitchy dance,
Unaware of the squirrels' prancing chance.
The woodpecker drills a rhythmic beat,
Creating a tune, oh, isn't it neat?

Flickering Flames Beneath the Fog

In the mist, a campfire glows,
Marshmallows float like little boats.
Ghosts of laughter swirl and spin,
While critters join the gathering din.

A raccoon dons a chef's tall hat,
Stirring up soup with a playful spat.
Chased by shadows that dance with glee,
They mock the moon, say, "Look at me!"

Requiem for the Rustling Roots

Roots that wiggle, roots that tease,
They laugh and giggle in the breeze.
Each tiny turn, a secret told,
Beneath the soil, it's a sight to behold.

Worms in tuxedos take their stance,
While little bugs join in the prance.
Nature's jesters, all in a line,
Digging and dancing, as they dine.

Phantoms of the Ponderosa

In the woods, the shadows dance,
A tree trunk tried to learn to prance.
It slipped on roots, fell with a thud,
And now it's telling jokes from the mud.

Squirrels gather for a nightly show,
With acorns as tickets, they're all in tow.
The giggles rise as the leaves shake,
'This tree's a comedian, make no mistake!'

Chilling Hymns of the Hollow Trunk

A hollow trunk hums a ghostly tune,
Aimless whispers in the light of the moon.
A raccoon joins in, with a tap on the bark,
'Now this is a jam, and I'm the spark!'

Owls chuckle softly, perched up high,
'Whooo's dancing? Oh, give it a try!'
The wind blows laughter through twisted vines,
Each rustle a punchline, all in good times.

Resonance of the Forgotten Forest

In a forest where the odd birds chuckle,
A turtle in sneakers starts to shuffle.
Toots of laughter from bushes and leaves,
As the turtle says, 'You'll never believe!'

A jazz band of owls and mice take the stage,
With beats so catchy, even trees engage.
Every branch is a maraca, every vine a string,
Who knew the woods could groove and sing?

Tales from the Twilight Thicket

In the thicket where shadows loom,
A ghostly cat makes quite the boom.
'Why do I scare? It's just my style!'
He winks and says, 'Stay awhile!'

A hedgehog rolls by, fashionably late,
'You missed the punchline!' he can't hesitate.
With laughter echoing through the trees,
Even the stars chuckle on the breeze.

The Forgotten Grove's Serenade

In shadows where the branches sway,
The lost squirrels dance and play.
Frogs wearing hats, quite out of line,
Croak about their favorite wine.

A ghostly owl with spectacles,
Read books on spectral reticles.
Whispers of leaves, a gossip spree,
While crickets chirp a symphony.

The moon, a jester, mocks the trees,
As shadows slap their barky knees.
The breeze brings chuckles from afar,
As fireflies twinkle like a star.

In this grove of ghoulish blight,
Even pumpkins laugh with all their might.
Join the party, all is well,
In the forgotten grove's sweet spell.

Phantasmal Sentinels of the Night

Old lanterns flicker with a grin,
Guardians of mischief and of sin.
They sway and giggle in soft delight,
As shadows chase away pure fright.

A phantom dog digs a ghostly hole,
What a wacky, mischievous soul!
With every bark, a laugh ensues,
Who knew spirits could be such a ruse?

The statues wink from mossy stones,
With cheesy jokes in hushed tones.
A mummified cat just laughed and hissed,
At the ghosts who nearly missed the twist.

If you wander these pathways strange,
Prepare for giggles, preposterous change.
For in the night, where spirits play,
Even shadows have their funny way.

The Twilight Watcher

Upon the hill where shadows blend,
A rascal crow is my good friend.
With a mischievous caw, he takes his stand,
Announcing tales of the snickering land.

The sun bows down, it's quite the sight,
While breezes strut and boast their might.
They tumble over roots, oh what a sight,
Tickling the grass with pure delight.

A raccoon in a top hat jives,
Stealing snacks as laughter thrives.
In twilight's glow, it's party time,
As critters coin their silly rhyme.

Here comes the moon, with a wink so bright,
Joining in on the whimsical night.
So come along, don't be a bore,
With each guffaw, we'll ask for more!

Conversation with the Graven Roots

Roots intertwine beneath the soil,
Chit-chatting as they twist and coil.
"Did you hear about the gopher's race?"
"They say he tripped and lost his pace!"

A wise old root, all gnarled and gray,
Chuckles nervously, clearing the way.
"Oh dear, let's not provoke the ants,
Last time they started a tiny dance!"

Stones rolled by with a playful tone,
"Join our party, don't sit alone!"
The whispers grow, a laughter fest,
In the underworld, it's quite the quest.

So here they share their grounded jest,
In a world where roots feel blessed.
From shadows deep, the laughter rings,
Among the buried, joy takes wings.

Solace in the Shaded Hollow

In the hollow where shadows play,
Squirrels throw acorns on a fray.
Ghosts in blankets of cobwebs stand,
Yet they dance to music from a band.

Bats wearing shades fly in a whirl,
While spiders spin tunes that make you twirl.
A raccoon juggles, oh what a sight,
Underneath the moon's gleaming light.

High above, owls with glasses squint,
Chatting gossip without a hint.
'Who wore it better,' they silently crow,
As the wind starts to hum with a flow.

In this grove where humor reigns,
Even the mist brings silly refrains.
Come join the fun, we won't take a fall,
In this shaded hollow, we laugh for all.

Beneath Haunting Branches

Beneath branches that reach for the sky,
A chipmunk whispers, 'Oh my, oh my!'
A funny ghost tickles the tree,
Saying, 'Laughter's the best remedy!'

Vines like ribbons sway and spin,
As creatures gather for a whim.
An owl in a bowtie leads the show,
With jokes that make the breezes blow.

The shadows giggle, what a delight,
While fireflies dance, shining bright.
They flash like stage lights, so wittily spry,
In this enchanted haunt where chuckles fly.

So take a seat on this gnarled root,
Join the shenanigans, give a hoot!
For beneath these branches, spooky yet sweet,
Laughter echoes, it can't be beat.

The Lament of the Misty Grove

In the misty grove, a frog croaks loud,
'This weather is weird, I'm feeling quite proud!'
A ghost in a tutu starts to twirl,
With little bats giggling in a whirl.

Leaves whisper secrets, they can't keep still,
Raccoons play tricks with abundant skill.
A misty fog holds their foolish pranks,
While trees shake their trunks and laugh in ranks.

Squirrels debate over acorn snacks,
'Is it gourmet or just grown-in cracks?'
Their serious squabble makes everyone grin,
As shadows join in, let the fun begin!

Oh, the laughter that floats in the air,
In this grove, joy is everywhere.
So heed the call of the funny and brave,
Join the spectacle that the spirits gave.

Echoing Through the Ages

In the twilight where chuckles dwell,
A comedy show from beneath the shell.
Ghosts with punchlines, each one a pro,
Make even the stones want to join the show.

Through ancient trunks, the echoes arise,
With snickers and giggles that reach for the skies.
A raccoon with a mic, takes center stage,
Spinning tall tales of a past age.

The branches sway, they can't keep quiet,
As laughter dances, a riotous diet.
A jolly old tree cracks a dad's funny,
'Why do spirits make pancakes? For the honey!'

In this gathering, shadows cavort,
Each chuckle and snort creates a rapport.
From the hoots to the cackles, joy is contagious,
In these hallowed woods where laughter is endless.

Reflections in Shadowed Glades

In the glade where shadows play,
Squirrels talk in a cheeky way.
Leaves giggle at the wind's delight,
As night creeps in, avoiding fright.

A rabbit trips, spills its tea,
'This isn't what I planned to be!'
Mice in coats waltz round the tree,
Is that a cat? Oh, woe is me!

Frogs jump high with a toad's cheers,
'We're the rulers of these spheres!'
They croak jokes, with leaps and bounds,
In these woods of playful sounds.

But when owls ask for a show,
They all freeze, quite scared, oh no!
With laughter hushed, they stand so still,
In shadows where giggles can't fulfill.

Terrors in the Thicket

In the thicket, whispers fright,
A raccoon dons a ghostly white.
'Boo!' he shouts, but a sly fox grins,
'This spooky game? Nope, it won't win.'

A hedgehog hides, all prickly and shy,
'I'm just a ball, do pass me by!'
The hedges murmur, they conspire,
While owls hold court, cooking up fire.

With every rustle, a tale unfurls,
Of grasshoppers ricocheting twirls.
An ant with a map tries to lead the way,
But lost, he just turns and yells, 'Hooray!'

Though shadows loom, there's no real fear,
Just woodland clowns spreading cheer.
In this thicket of playful lore,
Frights turn to laughter, forevermore.

A Last Lament for the Lost

Here lies a lost shoe by the brook,
Its partner's off exploring, the crook!
Toe tales are traded, 'They can't be found,'
While fish swim by, with giggles abound.

A hat floats down on a ladybug's head,
'I'm the queen!' she says, filled with dread.
But with a tilting crown, she prances around,
While crickets cheer with a jubilant sound.

An old sock sighs, 'I miss my mate,'
Yet ends up dancing with leaves—how great!
Sing laments for the things that roam,
Here they play, no need for a home.

With every joke, a memory we mend,
As shadows grow long, hearts on the bend.
In loss, find humor, life's fleeting jest,
In the hunt for lost things, we create our best.

Voices of the Ancient Ones

In whispers deep, the trees all talk,
What tales they share as shadows walk.
The ancients chuckle, their wisdom so sly,
'Who heard that noise? Just passin' by!'

A squirrel claims it knows the past,
While wise old owls hoot and laugh fast.
'Have you seen the moon? It's lost its glow!'
All the while, lightning bugs put on a show.

Mischief brewed, the wind sways tall,
Crickets click their legs for a ball.
'Who will dance; who'll take the stage?'
All join in a waltzing rage.

So listen close, for laughter hums,
In the breeze where the forest drums.
From tree to tree, let mirth cascade,
In this joyful world, no jest will fade.

Lurking in Dappled Light

In the glade where shadows play,
A squirrel danced the night away.
With acorns flung like tiny bombs,
He laughed and chirped—what joyful psalms!

A rabbit joined with a goofy hop,
Mistakenly thought—he's king, on top!
While the birds watched with curious eyes,
Of furry antics, oh what a prize!

A hedge maze turned into a race,
They tumbled down, oh what a face!
With dappled beams that softly blushed,
They giggled hard, then gently hushed.

Among the leaves, a rustle found,
Who knew that laughter could be such sound?
In dappled light, they'll always dwell,
Squirrels and rabbits weave quite the spell!

Ethereal Voices of the Forest

Whispers flit through branches high,
"Did you hear that?" echoes sigh.
A raccoon paused in sheer surprise,
Mischief glimmered in his eyes.

A wise old owl took to the floor,
"Please be quiet, I'm trying to snore!"
"Just a sec!" the chipmunk squeaked,
"As I unveil my new technique!"

The trees giggled, the leaves they danced,
Nature had given them a chance.
With jokes that echoed, soft and sweet,
The forest thrived on this silly beat.

And so the night, it filled with cheer,
As forest friends wrapped in their sphere.
Each twinkle held a story grand,
Where laughter reigned across the land!

Shade of Lost Memories

In the shadows, tales unwind,
Of cheeky sprites, and pranks in kind.
A gnome recites a tale so tall,
Of how he once caught a fish, that small!

A breeze carried gales of laughter bright,
As ladybugs tested their flight.
One tripped over a twig—oh dear!
The giggles echoed, loud and clear!

Underneath the sprawling trees,
The whispers danced with playful ease.
Where dreams and giggles intertwine,
Memories live in quirky design.

And every shade, a secret keeps,
Of woodland frolics and joyous leaps.
In twilight's hold, the critters scheme,
To keep alive the laughter's dream!

Shadows of the Past Whispered

Beneath the boughs, where whispers creep,
A ghostly figure begins to leap.
With spindly legs and a twisty grin,
He juggled mushrooms, oh what a sin!

A shadow in plaid, so very spry,
"Why did the chicken cross? Oh why?"
The trees snickered at the scene,
As laughter echoed—what a routine!

A bat swooped low, lost in a fit,
Of tickling the owl who wanted to sit.
"What year is it?" the owl surveyed,
In shadows of jokes, the past conveyed.

Each chuckle shared, a connecting thread,
As whispers of fun from the old days spread.
In darkened shades, where stories are spun,
The humor of time makes all of us one!

Whispers of Twilight's Embrace

In the twilight, weird creatures dance,
Squirrels in shadow, their little prance.
A raccoon wearing a tiny hat,
Claiming the moon for a chitchat chat.

The owls gossip in giggling tones,
As they share secrets of cheeky bones.
The stars twinkle with a knowing grin,
While bats glide by, wearing a sin.

Shades of the Rustling Past

Old trees chuckle with gnarled bark,
As the wind whispers secrets so stark.
A wise old crow, with glasses ajar,
Critiques the owls like a movie star.

The roots argue, they're not so deep,
As the squirrels plot and then start to leap.
The shadows quip, witty and bright,
Stealing the laughter from day to night.

Whispers Through the Wistful Woods

Woodland critters in a conga line,
Decide to hold parties at half-past nine.
The deer serve cupcakes, the fox plays drums,
While the hedgehogs giggle at jokes and puns.

The moonlight flickers like a jester's grin,
As every branch knows where the fun begins.
With every rustle, a punchline awaits,
Building a laughter that never abates.

Shadows Beneath the Ancient Boughs

Beneath the branches, shadows swirl,
Kittens and puppies in a playful twirl.
A disco party for woodland sprites,
Stomping and jumping, oh what a sight!

The stalwart tree, with wisdom so sly,
Offers advice with a wink of an eye.
While ghosts of squirrels just float and tease,
Foxtrots on leaves, just doing as they please.

Melodies in the Mist

In the fog where shadows dance,
A squirrel sings in pants and prance.
The owls giggle, lost in thought,
While wily winds blow jokes they've wrought.

A brook hums tunes of puddle sighs,
As frogs discuss the starry skies.
The trees drop leaves like silly hats,
And even crows wear rainbow spats.

The moon struts by with silver glee,
With a wink and nod, it prances free.
And whispers bounce through branches wide,
Where laughter hides and fun does bide.

So tiptoe softly, do not tease,
The giggling mist beneath the trees.
For every rustle's playful jest,
Is nature's way of having zest.

The Enchanted Wood's Sigh

In a glade where ferns and flowers bloom,
A gnome picks fights with a broom.
He scoffs at leaves that swirl and spin,
While squirrels cheer for his silly win.

The breeze carries whispers of fun,
As badger chases a glimmering bun.
Twirling mushrooms sing off-key,
While a tortoise struts with giddy glee.

The shadows tease the timid deer,
With silly grins that bring good cheer.
The brook rolls laughter, bubbling bright,
While crickets croon into the night.

So come, my friend, and take a peek,
At nature's giggles, so unique.
For in this realm of whimsy's flight,
Every moment is pure delight.

Enigma of the Lingering Shade

A shadow whispers with a grin,
Playing tricks on passersby skin.
It teases leaves, it twirls around,
And makes them dance upon the ground.

A cat with hat schemes mischief bright,
While owls wink at the moon's soft light.
The lizards laugh with giddy glee,
Their tails a-swirl, they dare to flee.

The wind tells tales of jesters past,
Of echoes swirling, oh so fast.
And as the stars begin to glow,
The laughter rises, soft and low.

So linger here, where shadows play,
And join in jest before the day.
For in this realm of twilight's shade,
The jokes of night shall never fade.

Spirits of the Verdant Vale

In a vale where spirits roam and jest,
They play hide and seek, never let rest.
With shimmery giggles, they glide through trees,
Tickling leaves, dancing in the breeze.

A fox in a tux, sharp as a tack,
Performs magic tricks from a leafy stack.
While rabbits chant in a merry choir,
Their joyful songs never tire.

The berries blush with giggly delight,
As mushrooms giggle deep in the night.
The owls hoot riddles, perplexing and fun,
While butterflies chase the setting sun.

So wander and wonder, come join the spree,
In this vale of spirits, wild and free.
For laughter echoes in every glade,
A celebration that'll never fade.

The Dance of Shadows

In moonlight's glow, they prance and sway,
Goblins in masks just love to play.
A waltz of whispers spins so low,
While shadow friends steal the show.

With feet so light, they stomp around,
Creating mischief without a sound.
A dance-off starts, who's got the flair?
The tree just giggles, branches in the air.

Watch out for roots, they're out to trip,
Gnarled and twisted, like an acrobat's slip.
The moon can't help but laugh with glee,
As shadows spin, wild and free.

With every step, a joke prevails,
As owls hoot laughter, telling tales.
The forest joins in a merry jest,
Where even the night feels quite blessed.

Nightfall's Reluctant Embrace

As night creeps in, the stars complain,
"Must we be stuck in this dark domain?"
The moon rolls eyes, says with a chuckle,
"It's just a phase, don't burst your bubble!"

The night fights back, whispers so sly,
"Don't fret, dear stars, we'll let dreams fly!"
Yet shadows giggle, a hare in flight,
"Did you just see a monster? Oh, what a fright!"

A breeze sneezes through branches so high,
The leaves all shudder, "Was that a sigh?"
But in the dark, whimsy does bloom,
With creatures of night, dispelling the gloom.

So when you think of night's embrace,
Just remember laughter fills the space.
For every eerie nook you find,
There's humor hiding, ever so kind.

The Solitary Stump's Tale

Once a tree with branches so wide,
Now a stump with nowhere to hide.
"Just call me Gary," it says with pride,
"Though I miss my leaves, I won't subside!"

With squirrels that come to crack a joke,
And butterflies swirling like a colorful cloak.
They mock his height, but he laughs back,
"Just means I'm grounded, on a different track!"

The birds serenade him, oh what a show,
"A stump with flair, let the fun flow!"
With each tale told, he's quite a delight,
The king of puns in the moonlit night.

So next time you find a stump in your way,
Give it a chuckle, don't turn away.
For Gary's got stories that never run dry,
In a forest where laughter will always fly.

Chilling Breeze Through Hollow Boughs

A breeze whispers secrets, tickles the ears,
While wooden folks giggle, easing fears.
"What's that?" sighs the willow so grand,
"A ghost? Or just breeze? Let's make a stand!"

The oaks are chattering, sharing their lore,
Of that one night a squirrel ran out the door.
"A ghost stole my acorns!" cried a loud shriek,
Turns out it was just a clever old beak!

The branches sway, a comedic dance,
While shadows play games in the moonlit lance.
A howl in the distance starts quite the cheer,
Two foxes debating —"Did you see that deer?"

So if you hear laughter among the trees,
Just know it's the whispers bringing you peace.
For in every corner where shadows roam,
There's a chuckle or two, and a sense of home.

Enchanted Whispers in the Gloom

Beneath a branch, a squirrel did prance,
With nuts aplenty, plotting his chance.
He tried to dance, but slipped on a prank,
Fell in a puddle, oh what a clank!

The owls hooted, a wise old crew,
"His ballet skills? A bit askew!"
The wind laughed softly, as leaves took flight,
"Mistakes are magic, so take to the night!"

Ghostly figures peeked through the haze,
Chuckling softly, weaving their maze.
Each shadow flickered, a jokester's game,
In the gloom, they whispered, "What's in a name?"

A rustle here, a giggle there,
While branches bowed, with graceful flair.
Laughter hung like dew in the air,
Oh, the wonders of the woodland fair!

The Solitary Oak's Reverie

In a meadow stood an oak so tall,
Wishing for friends, he felt so small.
But every critter dashed away in fright,
"Too many branches! It's quite a sight!"

He sighed aloud, with a ponderous frown,
"Are my limbs too large for this old town?"
Yet, passing squirrels couldn't help but tease,
"Your beard's a tangle, it tickles the breeze!"

Moonlit nights brought critter debates,
About the finest of nutty traits.
The oak just chuckled, "As I stand alone,
My shadow's grand, and my laughs are known!"

In solitude, he found his glee,
Dancing with shadows, wild and free.
Who needs a crowd when you're this bold?
A tree with tales of laughter retold!

A Grove Shrouded in Mystery

In a grove where giggles whisper and sway,
A tree with secrets in shadows does play.
With vines that twist in a playful dance,
Who knew old roots could take a chance?

The breeze stirred rumors of sprites so bright,
That pranked the moon on a mischievous night.
"Who's that giggling?" a traveler sighed,
"The trees are laughing, they've nothing to hide!"

A rabbit looked up with a curious ear,
"Did I hear chuckles? Come near, come near!"
With twinkling eyes and a fluff of a tail,
He joined the laughter, they all set sail.

In this place where the weird is quite grand,
Every branch has a tale, every twig knows a band.
So join in the fun, let your worries depart,
For the grove sings laughter, a delightful art!

Phantoms of the Forgotten Arboreal

In a forest deep where the fog likes to play,
Phantoms arise at the end of the day.
They flip through the leaves, with a rustle and cheer,
"Join our parade, there's nothing to fear!"

With branches like arms, they twirl in delight,
Booing and laughing, they dance in the night.
A ghost with a grin caught a firefly bold,
"Come shine with us, let your stories be told!"

Around twinkling mushrooms, a party took form,
With spirits and wonders, a mythical swarm.
They shared silly tales of the trees from the past,
Laughter echoed loudly, a spell that would last.

So if you should wander where branches entwine,
Remember the phantoms, their laughter divine.
In the moonlight, they'll beckon, a whimsical show,
Join in the fun, let your spirit glow!

Phantoms Among the Branches

In the night, a ghostly sight,
Doing a jig under pale moonlight.
With a wig made of leaves so green,
Dancing wildly, unseen, obscene.

They trip over roots, oh what a blast,
They giggle and laugh, forgetting the past.
One fell down, the others all squealed,
'Next time, we must wear a shield!'

A squirrel stopped, stared in surprise,
At spectral friends with glowing eyes.
Then a crow cawed, 'What's all this fun?'
The phantoms replied, 'Just out for a run!'

Then suddenly poof, they vanished in air,
Leaving the night with a faint flair.
The squirrel just shrugged, 'I've seen stranger,
Like the time I lost a nut to a danger!'

The Old Sentinel's Cry

Ancient bark with secrets to tell,
Whispers of mischief, all is well.
With branches like arms, it stretches wide,
Cracking jokes, it cannot hide.

'Why do trees never play poker?' it mused,
'Because they might get trunk-accused!'
A chipmunk giggled, fell from a branch,
'Thank you, dear tree, for this chance!'

The night wore on with raucous delight,
As the old sentinel shared more fright.
'What's a tree's favorite drink, my friend?'
'A-root beer!' It laughed without end.

Yet with each laugh, a rustle intrudes,
As shadows conspire in playful moods.
'Now that's a twist!' the tree did yell,
'Time for a tale that's sure to compel!'

Beneath the Leafy Veil

Beneath the shade where secrets creep,
A gnome snores softly, lost in sleep.
Swaying branches rock him slow,
While leaf-shaped dreams put on a show.

Suddenly, a frog leaps in surprise,
'Can you keep it down?' it shouts and cries.
Nature chuckled, softly shook,
Even the flowers in corners took a look.

The gnome awoke, grumbled a tune,
'Who woke me up? It wasn't the moon!'
A wise old owl with a wink said,
'Sometimes your dreams need a little spread.'

So he leapt up, danced a jig,
With colors so bright, he'd wear a wig!
Under the leaf's shimmering grace,
Even the sun couldn't help but embrace.

Murmurs of Forgotten Souls

In the twilight, shadows prance,
Forgotten souls take a chance.
With a flicker and a goofy grin,
They're here to throw a spooky spin.

'Knock knock!' they call, with a ghostly cheer,
'Who's there?' replied a bat, full of fear.
'Orange!' they said, with a mischievous spin,
'Orange you glad we let you in?'

A howl erupted, laughter ensued,
As the ghosts played tricks, a jolly brood.
'Let's scare some folks!' one spirit did cry,
But only managed a silly, soft sigh.

In the end, they shared ghost stories grand,
While sipping on dew in the moonlit land.
For beneath all the fright, they found it was clear,
That laughter and joy are what ghosts hold dear!

Songs of the Shrouded Sycamore

In the shadows, squirrels scheme,
With acorns and a sneaky dream.
They chatter loud, like little pranks,
Creating chaos by the banks.

Branches sway with silly grace,
As birds all try to find their place.
A robin giggles at a crow,
"Why wear black? Just let it go!"

Leaves play tricks with autumn's dance,
Falling down, they take a chance.
A gust of wind, they twirl and twine,
As if they're all part of a line.

So underneath this wide expanse,
Nature sends us into a trance.
With laughter wrapped in leafy tunes,
We're just as silly as the loons.

Shadows Danced in the Dusk

Dusk descends with a cheeky grin,
Where the shadows start to spin.
A raccoon prances in the light,
With an acorn hat, oh what a sight!

Mice in tuxedos take the floor,
Swinging hard till they hit the door.
Chirping crickets call the beat,
While fireflies flash, oh what a feat!

A whispering breeze joins the ball,
Turning tall trees into a hall.
Each flickering glow makes hearts swell,
As laughter rings like a magic spell.

Oh, shadows dance through the cool night air,
Spreading joy without a care.
And if you listen, you might find,
That evening's fun is quite unkind!

Whispers on the Windy Trail

On the trail where the wild things sing,
The breeze covers everything.
A squirrel stops to have a chat,
"Have you heard about that hat?"

The winds carry tales with a tease,
Of owls who laugh and dance with ease.
A buzzing bee breaks into song,
"Come dance with me, please don't be long!"

Leaves gossip softly at the start,
Sharing secrets, they feel so smart.
A mouse jokes, "I lost my shoe!"
As laughter ripples past the blue.

And as the twilight paints the scene,
Nature laughs, all bright and keen.
With whispers weaving through the trails,
Life's a funny tale that never fails.

The Lonesome Lore of the Leaf

A leaf fell down with quite a thud,
Said, "I'm free! Look at this crud!"
It rolled and bounced on the soft ground,
Proclaiming joy with every round.

A worm looked up, quite confused,
"Why so jolly? You seem amused!"
"I'm off to see the world anew,
Join me, friend, there's fun for two!"

Together they ventured far and wide,
With giggles echoing in every stride.
The leaf and worm played hide and seek,
In grassy fields, cheeky and sleek.

As the sunset painted the day,
They laughed and danced in playful sway.
For a leaf and worm can truly glean,
Life's a jest, bright and serene!

The Unseen Keeper of the Grove

In the shade where shadows play,
Squirrels chatter, come what may.
A guardian with a silly grin,
He's lost his hat, where to begin?

The rabbits giggle, soft and spry,
They tiptoe round, oh me, oh my!
With acorns dropped and giggles burst,
In this hillock, mischief's first.

Dancing mushrooms, wiggle and sway,
Pretending they're boogieing night and day.
In a wine bottle, they found a friend,
It's quite a party that seems to never end!

Beneath the branches, secrets tease,
The keeper chuckles, "More than a breeze!"
Mice are sculpting tales anew,
Starring the woods, and silly too!

Dances of Dust and Leaves

A leaf twirls up, a pirouette grand,
With a whispering waltz, as if planned.
It tickles a twig, a tiny charade,
While crickets laugh, into the glade.

The dust motes shimmer, in sunlit rounds,
As beetles march to invisible sounds.
With twigs for sticks, they form a band,
Singing a song that's beautifully bland.

Owls in the night throw a shadowy rave,
With owlets dancing, so brave and so sprave.
"Whooo" goes the horn, their call so bright,
It's a party beneath the starlit night!

As twilight giggles, the moon dips low,
The steps of the critters begin to flow.
In a swirl of laughter, they all unite,
In nature's concert, pure delight!

Beneath the Aged Canopy

Under branches, wise and wide,
A raccoon dons a cloak, oh what a ride!
He sways to tunes of the whispering breeze,
A funny encore with acorn keys.

The shadows flicker with fairy lights,
Among the toadstools, they share delights.
"More tea, dear friends?" a hedgehog calls,
As laughter echoes in the stone-walled halls.

A gnome peeks out, his beard so grand,
Behind a fern, with a mug in hand.
He twists with joy, at every joke,
His laughter's hearty, like whiffs of smoke.

Mole plays chess with a sleepy cat,
Who's winning? Oh, nobody knows that!
In a world where nonsense blooms,
Joy dances softly, in darkened rooms.

A Note in the Wind

A whisper rides upon the breeze,
Scribbled secrets in the trees.
A tiny note floats, what does it say?
"Who left these fruitcakes in disarray?"

The cardinals caw in melodic spree,
As they decipher nature's decree.
"What's for lunch? Acorn pie?"
The wind laughs lightly and sweeps on by.

A foghorn toad croaks, "Let's make a plan!
We'll bake some muffins, yes we can!"
While buzzing bees buzz in delight,
Singing sweet nothings into the night.

Fallen leaves join in, waving hello,
As nature's friends put on a show.
A whispered laugh, a fluttering sound,
In this enchanting playground, joy abounds!

Echoing Through Decades

In the shade of branches wide,
A squirrel wore my sweater, tried.
He looked so dapper, I couldn't lie,
He danced around, oh my, oh my!

A ghost with glasses, sipping tea,
Claims he'd known me when I was three.
He tells the tales of all my blunders,
While I just sit and laugh like thunder.

The tree itself seems quite amused,
As birds debate who's been confused.
"Not my fault!" they chirp in jest,
While falling leaves join in the fest.

Around this haunt, I chuckle loud,
With every twig that snaps, I'm proud.
For laughter lifts the twilight gloom,
And makes the night a funny room.

The Lonely Light Beneath the Boughs

A lantern hangs, all by its lonesome,
It tells jokes to shadows, so seldom.
"Why did the branch refuse to speak?
Because it knew some trees were weak!"

Beneath the boughs, a weird old man,
Claims he's a part of nature's plan.
He whispers to owls, gives frogs advice,
"Always read the moon, it's quite precise!"

The laughter rises with the fog,
As squirrels giggle at a lost dog.
"What brings you here, old mutt, so mild?"
"I'm searching for a treehouse, child!"

Yet here we dwell, in joyful fright,
With every ripple of the night.
For mischief hides among the leaves,
In this bright corner, laughter weaves.

Traces of the Unseen

A raccoon with a top hat strolls,
And says, "I'm off to steal some coals!"
He winks at me, a gentle tease,
"Join me, friend, we'll grab some cheese!"

Hushed whispers from the branches sway,
A duet of leaves as they play.
"See that broomstick? It's going abroad,
I heard it's off to play with a frog!"

Behind the bark, a giggling sprite,
Dances barefoot in the moonlight.
"Who needs a crown when you've got a hat?
I'm the queen of the furry and chubby cat!"

I chuckle at this forest crew,
Each hidden trip's a delight anew.
For beneath this trickling stream,
Lies a land alive with whimsical dreams.

Flickers of Lost Time

Time flickers like a firefly's flight,
Chasing laughter into the night.
"Let's rewind," says a chipmunk bold,
As he recounts tales of ancient gold.

Fleeting moments dance in the breeze,
As spiders spin their webs with ease.
"Why do we sing?" a beetle inquires,
"To tune our hearts to the growing choirs!"

A clock in the branches ticks away,
Saying, "Hurry, don't let joy decay!"
Whispers float on the winds so light,
"Let's stay a while, it feels just right!"

Each second shared beneath these trees,
Brings warmth and joy, a gentle tease.
For in the echoes of laughter's rhyme,
We find the flickers of lost time.

Secrets of the Twilight Wood

In shadows deep, where whispers dance,
The squirrels plot their grand romance.
A raccoon croons a midnight tune,
While owls laugh by the light of the moon.

The rabbits hold a poker night,
With carrots stacked in comical fright.
They wager nuts on who'll be fast,
While shadows stretch and laughter lasts.

Strange creatures gather, wearing hats,
Juggling acorns, and fancy mats.
A fox slips on a shinny leaf,
And lands in laughter, much to his grief.

With secrets nestled in each nook,
The twilight wood's a comic book.
Where every rustle, every call,
Is filled with joy, and fun for all.

The Singing Tree's Secret

In the grove where the breezes hum,
A tree has found a way to strum.
With branches plucking leaves like strings,
It serenades the squirrels' flings.

A bird will chip in with a tweet,
As chipmunks tap their tiny feet.
They gather round for concert night,
In the glow of fireflies so bright.

But one shy mushroom wants to sing,
It opens wide, gives it a fling.
A croak so loud, it scares a deer,
All the critters burst out in cheer.

Laughter rings through every bough,
As laughter folds into each vow.
The singing don't stop, it's quite a feat,
Where rhythm makes the woodland beat.

Murmurings of the Underbrush

In tangled weeds, they gather near,
A committee of ants, full of cheer.
With tiny plans and grand designs,
They'll build a fort from sticks and twines.

A snail looks on, munching his leaf,
Chiming in with a slow, wise belief.
"Why hurry friends? The day is vast!
Let's chew on dreams, and have a blast!"

Beetles roll balls just for fun,
While grasshoppers hop, not on the run.
They play leapfrog, and giggle with glee,
The underbrush a carnival spree.

Amid the chaos, a worm gives a shout,
"Let's have a race, there's no doubt!"
The world below's no place for fear,
Just silly tricks and hearty cheer.

Cries of the Timeworn Trunks

Beneath the boughs of ancient lore,
The trees hold tales of yawn and snore.
They creak and groan at the slightest breeze,
Whispering jokes that tickle their knees.

A bark beetle shouts, "Tell us more!"
With tales of branches and wacky decor.
"A squirrel once dressed in a leaf so green,
He started a trend, it was quite the scene!"

The trunks trade stories, both silly and bold,
Of acorn feasts and mischief untold.
They reminisce about windy days,
When tumbleweeds danced in oddly shaped ways.

So gather 'round, hear their playful cries,
In the heart of the wood, where laughter lies.
While nature's secrets swirl and twine,
The old trees remind us—it's all divine!

The Haunting Rustle of Leaves

A squirrel in a top hat, so dapper and neat,
Dancing with the shadows, tapping his feet.
The leaves laugh along, with a rustling cheer,
As the moon winks softly, bringing up the rear.

Branches stretch out, in a comical pose,
Tickling the night breeze, with fingers like toes.
A rustle, a giggle, in the cool autumn air,
As owls hoot their jokes, without any care.

The wind whispers secrets, a joke it has curled,
Lorcan the ghost cat, in a flurry, is twirled.
Chasing after shadows, he trips on a root,
And tumbles down softly, oh what a hoot!

So dance with the night, let laughter abound,
In the rustle of leaves, silly joy can be found.
For who knew the forest could be such a tease?
With critters in costumes, rustling with ease.

Silhouettes at Dusk

As the sun dips low, the shadows take flight,
Here comes a tall figure, dressed all in white.
'Not a ghost!' It declares, 'Just a waiter in guise,
Serving laughs from the dusk, with a side of surprise!'

Then a rabbit in glasses, reading a map,
Lost in the woods, oh what a mishap!
He sighs, 'Just my luck!' as he fumbles around,
While the trees start to giggle, without making sound.

A frog on a log croaks, 'I'm all dressed to kill!'
In a tuxedo made of leaves, he sits very still.
He plans a grand ball for the critters at night,
Where even the moonbeams will twirl in delight!

From the corners of twilight, the silliness peeks,
As figures sway softly, with whispers and squeaks.
So join in the fun, as shadows unite,
In the mismatched parade of the wacky twilight.

Whispers from the Roots

Beneath the tall trunks, where the weird things grow,
Roots gossip and chatter in a whispery flow.
'Did you hear about Daisy, who wears mismatched shoes?

She danced with the gophers and sang to the blues!'

Moles in their burrows chuckle and snicker,
'And Timmy the toad? He's a wizard with flicker!'
They hold magic meetings, with acorns for tea,
Debating if tree bark tastes better with brie.

Then come the old vines, with stories to tell,
About squirrels in chariots, racing down from the dell.
They've got tales of mischief, of pranks gone awry,
A woodpecker's drumming, that made big trees cry!

So lean down to listen, tucked under a leaf,
The roots' rib-tickling tales, bring laughter and relief.
For in the dark soil, where the whispers spin,
Lies a world of delight, where the nonsense begins.

Forest of Unseen Faces

In the forest of shadows, where the funny things dwell,
The branches play peek-a-boo, wishing you well.
'Oh, look at our friend! Are those eyes on that trunk?'
A face in the bark, just a little bit punk!

With grins made of moss and a smile wide as day,
The trees throw a party, 'Come join us and play!'
Underneath ferns, where the whispers are keen,
They spin silly stories from the grass's green sheen.

The flowers all giggle, in their colorful attire,
While bees dance around them, like they're a live choir.
Each petal a laugh, each blossom a tease,
In the forest of faces, where fun's sure to please!

So follow the giggles, let your heart take delight,
In the bustling woods where even shadows are bright.
For here in the laughter, the unseen will show,
That whimsy's a treasure, just waiting to grow!

Twilight Tales of the Tendril Trees

In twilight's grasp, the branches twirl,
Leaves whisper secrets, like an old girl.
A squirrel in a tux, he steals the show,
Chorruping jokes in the warm glow.

Mossy mushrooms don't take a nap,
They dance with shadows, a funky clap.
An owl wears glasses, looking quite wise,
While bats play cards, oh what a surprise!

Raccoons in capes, they strike a pose,
With pine cone crowns, the forest's heroes.
Each rustling branch, a chuckle shared,
As tree trunks giggle, they're duly prepared.

So gather around, hear nature's jest,
Under the boughs where humor's at its best.
The woods are alive with laughter and cheer,
Join in the fun, have no fear!

Lament of the Loneliest Oak

There once was an oak, so dreadfully tall,
He stood all alone, felt so very small.
His branches were heavy with sighs of the past,
He longed for a friend, but none came at last.

A rabbit hopped by, wearing a hat,
Said, "Hey big fella, don't sit like a mat!"
"Let's play hide and seek, come join in the fun,"
But the oak just sighed, said, "Oh, I'm not one!"

Then came a parrot, so chatty and bright,
With puns in his beak, he filled up the night.
The oak had to chuckle, it tickled his bark,
His loneliness slipped like a lark in the dark.

So now he's the king of this comedic spree,
With forest friends laughing, so wild and free.
The sun sets gently, shadows retrieve,
And the loneliest oak learns to believe.

Specters in the Saplings

In moonlit groves, the saplings sway,
With giggles and whispers, they dance and play.
Tiny ghouls in cozy hoods,
Plot mischief under the starry woods.

One pretends to trip on a fallen leaf,
"Oh dear! I'm stuck!"—a playful thief!
The others laugh in their ghostly tones,
As branches shake with their puppy moans.

A ghost with a bowtie tells a tall tale,
About how he tried to ride a snail.
With antics like this, who'd ever be scared?
Not a single tree bark's feeling impaired!

So if you wander where shadows loom,
Listen closely, you might hear their tune.
Laughter in nature, it's not what it seems,
In a world made of whispers, and strange little dreams.

Ghostly Glimmers in the Gloom

When dusk descends and shadows creep,
Ghostly glimmers wake from sleep.
With laughter loud, they tickle the breeze,
Playing peek-a-boo behind the trees.

A lantern bug sings his favorite song,
While shadows sway, they dance along.
Old branches creak, join in the fun,
As nightfall's clock strikes two, then one.

A wisp in a tutu spins while it twirls,
With spindly fingers, it twirls and swirls.
"Come join us!" they shout, "Leave your worries behind,"

In the gnarled gloom where sweet joy's entwined.

So if you wander in this twilight gleam,
Expect to laugh, it's not just a dream.
For friendly phantoms and shimmering light,
Bring a chuckle to every night.

Legend of the Whispering Wood

In the woods where shadows play,
A squirrel claims he's lost his way.
He chats with trees, both tall and grand,
While branches laugh, they'll take a stand.

The owls wear glasses, quite absurd,
They gossip softly, every word.
A rabbit thinks he's quite the sage,
But all he does is dance and rage.

The moonlight dances on the leaves,
While crickets knit their evening sleeves.
With every rustle, jokes abound,
In this odd place where fun is found.

So if you wander, heed this call,
Listen closely, have a ball.
For in this wood of whispered cheer,
You might just find a friend or near.

Parables of the Bark and Branch

The branches chatter, wise and spry,
"Why did the twig refuse to fly?"
"Because," they shout with laughter bright,
"He knew he'd fall without a fight!"

A beetle boasts of strength and size,
While ants just roll their tiny eyes.
The bark tells tales of silly falls,
As mushrooms giggle, heed their calls.

A wandering fox with hat askew,
Pretends to read a book or two.
But all it does is snore away,
While bushes whisper, "What a day!"

In this grove of jests and glee,
Even the wind joins in, you see.
From root to crown, the laughter spans,
Among this crowd of leafy fans.

Secrets of the Mossy Floor

Upon the ground, where secrets lie,
A toad sits munching on a fly.
He croaks a tune of pure delight,
While butterflies take graceful flight.

The mossy patches dance with glee,
As worms recite a comedy.
Each slither brings a chuckle low,
These hidden halls where jesters grow.

A raccoon juggles acorns round,
While sunbeams sneak without a sound.
The mushrooms clap, a cheerful crowd,
In this soft place, no worries loud.

So tiptoe here, embrace the sill,
Let nature's winks give you a thrill.
For every corner holds a tale,
Where laughter echoes, never pale.

The Silent Oak's Refrain

A noble oak stands, quiet, wise,
With squirrels plotting small disguise.
They stage a play, all nutty themes,
While leaves applaud with rustling screams.

A chipmunk plays a tiny flute,
While acorns roll in evening's suit.
The buzzards gossip from on high,
As shadows shift and dreams supply.

The silent oak, with humor vast,
Keeps secrets close, from first to last.
Each knot and twist, a giggle stored,
Through seasons passed, the joy adored.

So gather near, when dusk descends,
And let the tree share jokes with friends.
In this grand space of merry throng,
Life's little quirks will carry on.

Secrets Beneath the Starry Canopy

Beneath the stars, the squirrels prance,
Seeking nuts in a silly dance.
The moonlight giggles, the night owls cheer,
Who knew the woods could be so dear?

Tangled branches whisper their jokes,
As fireflies twinkle, dressed like folks.
A raccoon winks, tips his hat fine,
Under the canopy, we sip on pine wine.

The shadows hide some cheeky ghouls,
Playing tricks, those wily fools.
With a rustle and cackle, they make their round,
In this leafy carnival, fun's easily found.

The trees sway low, a playful sway,
Inviting all to come out and play.
Laughter echoes in the crisp night air,
For in this secret world, there's joy to share.

Forests Sing of Solitude

Amidst the trees, a lone fox sneaks,
With clumsy steps and silly squeaks.
He tries to dance, but trips in glee,
The forest chuckles—just wait and see!

Leaves fall down with a gentle thud,
Landing softly in a fluffy mud.
Frogs croak songs with an offbeat tune,
Who knew solitude had such a boon?

Twilight's glow starts to tease the night,
A shadow juggles, oh what a sight!
With a giggle and wiggle, the owl turns round,
Turning this quiet to merry sound.

Each rustle brings a tale to tell,
Of lonely souls who know it well.
In their hush, there's a knack for fun,
Even solitude can't be outdone!

Sighs of the Selkie Grove

In a grove where the playful selkies swim,
Their laughter echoes, a whimsical hymn.
With fishy winks and twirls galore,
They flop and slide, begging for more.

The old trees nod, draped in moss,
Shaking their branches, what a toss!
Selkies giggle, with splashes like pies,
Even the night sky can't hide its sighs.

A mist comes in, friendly yet coy,
As selkies craft a game, oh boy!
They leap from waves in a slippery sport,
Turning the pond into a splashy court.

With a flick and a flop, the laughter grows,
As bubbles rise from their silly shows.
In this grove where mischief thrives,
It's where the joyful, fidgeting selkies come alive!

Sable Shadows of the Silent Depths

In the depths, where shadows twine,
Silent giggles dance on vine.
A creature grins, with a twist of fate,
It's a catfish laughing—it's never late!

The water shimmers with chuckles low,
As fish parade, all in a row.
They twin and swirl in a grand ballet,
Each ripple adds to the funny play.

A beaver's slid past with a splashy sound,
Creating waves that bounce all around.
With bobbing tails and silly grins,
This underwater world surely wins!

Each shadow's deep but full of cheer,
Where laughter echoes crystal clear.
In the sable depths, under the moon's light,
The creatures jive till the dawn's first sight!

Lurking Beneath the Bark

Beneath the old tree's creak and groan,
A squirrel plots to claim a throne.
With acorns stacked and nuts galore,
He'll rule the yard, forevermore!

The shadows dance, the leaves they sway,
A raccoon joins the nutty fray.
'No crown for you!' the squirrel squeaks,
As laughter fills the forest peaks.

A wise old owl gives side-eye grace,
To witness this chaotic race.
With every bindle, bicker, and brawl,
Who knew a tree could hold it all?

The wind starts laughing with a twirl,
As leaves laugh too in jigs and whirl.
While all around, the humor's stark,
We dance and sing beneath the bark.

Nightfall's Silent Shroud

When night descends with sly invites,
The crickets sing their quirky rites.
The moon, a grin, peeks through the leaves,
As laughter drapes like spider weaves.

A shadow alights, a misplaced toe,
A ghostly sneeze disrupts the show.
'Bless you!' calls a fairy in chime,
As bursts of giggles flip through time.

When owls hoot, it's not despair,
But chat about their feathery flair.
Raccoons await for late-night feasts,
With jokes on mischief, they are beasts!

The night is thick with silly dreams,
Where nothing's ever as it seems.
Wrapped in a shroud of laughter bright,
The dark reveals its comedic light.

The Ghostly Chorus of Twilight

At dusk, when shadows play and sway,
A chorus starts its funny fray.
'Boo!' they shout, in comical fright,
As giggles echo through the night!

The phantom on the swing lets fly,
A ticklish breeze, he'll not deny.
With juggling orbs and moonlit pies,
They put the silliest in disguise.

A waltzing bat, so light on wing,
Can't resist to join and swing.
'You call that a dance?' a firefly blinks,
As lantern insects laugh in sync.

With whimsy wrapped in twilight's glow,
The spirits cast their banter flow.
They lift the night, spark joy anew,
In jest and laugh, we drift on through.

Twilit Dreams of the Ancient Arbor

As twilight falls, the branches spin,
With whispered tales of where we've been.
A gnome with glasses, sipping tea,
Says, 'Life's too short for woes, oh me!'

The branches creak with giggling sprites,
Who jump and leap through dreamy flights.
They trade their jokes for moonlight treats,
Where every line a chuckle greets.

In every shadow, mischief gleams,
Like silly plots from childhood dreams.
An ancient tree with bark like quilt,
Holds memories of laughter built.

So dance along the forest's floor,
As twilight whispers evermore.
With playful glimmers and cheeky charms,
The arbor warms us in its arms.

Secrets of the Silvery Grove

In the grove where whispers play,
Squirrels sport in a silly way.
They chatter loud, making a fuss,
While raccoons dance, oh what a plus!

The shadows stretch, they twist and bow,
A playful breeze makes branches wow.
A joke is told by the wind's soft sigh,
While owls roll eyes as bats fly by.

Leaves giggle as they spin around,
Painting the air without a sound.
The trees, they laugh in leafy cheer,
As twilight spills its light most clear.

So take a stroll 'neath silver beams,
Where nature's laughter forms the dreams.
In this grove, the night is bright,
With every rustle, pure delight!

Murmurs in the Moonlit Canopy

Under the moon, a chatter rings,
Where shadows dance on tiny wings.
A frog croaks jokes, a toad sings high,
As fireflies blip and winks they fly.

A wise old owl gives sage advice,
While raccoons roll the dice, so nice!
The branches sway with playful grace,
Unbeknownst to the bushes' face.

Laughter tumbles from the leaves,
As crickets play their romping thieves.
The night wears laughter like a crown,
In this moonlit world of ups and downs.

So join the fun in the shimmering night,
As the forest cheers in pure delight.
For every critter has a part,
In merry songs that warm the heart!

Lurking Beneath the Leafless Limbs

Under limbs so stark and bare,
Goblins peek with mischief flair.
In their hats, they keep a stash,
Of tricks and treats, a joyful splash!

The owl, a prankster wise and sly,
Would wink at passers, oh so spry.
The wind would giggle, tickle the trees,
As laughter danced upon the breeze.

A fox in boots struts with pride,
While nearby, a porcupine tries to hide.
Beneath the bark, a joke does creep,
With every rustle, secrets sleep.

So venture forth beneath those limbs,
Where the light leaps and the fun begins.
For in the dark, the laughter swells,
In leafy tales, our spirit dwells!

The Haunting Heartbeat of the Forest

In the heart of woodlands deep,
The trees giggle, and the owls leap.
With a pulse of laughter, they thrum along,
Join in the rhythm, a whimsical song.

Spiders spin webs of ticklish threads,
As mushrooms dance on tiny heads.
The heart's a drum of fun and glee,
Where shadowed shapes play hide and seek.

Whimsical winds whistle their tune,
In a chorus bright as a summer's moon.
A bear in a bow tie prances about,
Singing songs that make you shout.

So listen close, let spirits rise,
In haunted ha-has beneath the skies.
With every heartbeat, joy unfolds,
In stories of laughter, bravely told!

www.ingramcontent.com/pod-product-compliance
Lightning Source LLC
Chambersburg PA
CBHW051628160426
43209CB00004B/565